What is a Dinosaur?

Dinosaurs roamed the Earth a long, long time ago. The word dinosaur means "monstrous lizard." Dinosaurs were some of the largest animals ever to walk on Earth! Some dinosaurs ate plants and others ate meat.

DINO BITE:

Dinosaurs were bigger than elephants!

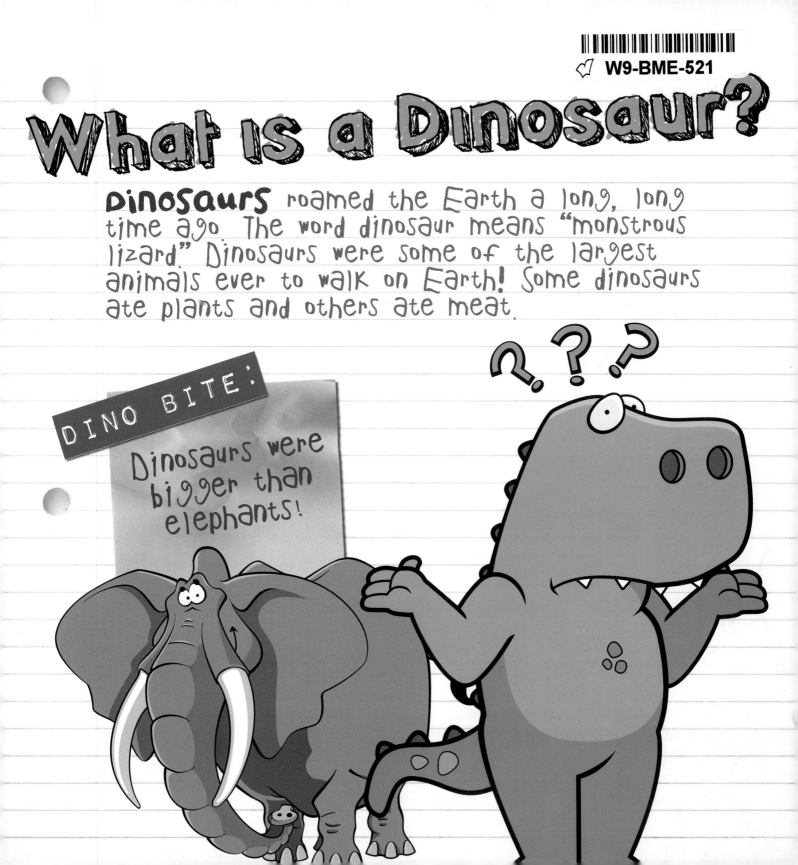

Dinosaur Timeline

Dinosaurs lived on Earth for about 165 million years. But they suddenly became **extinct** 65 million years ago. Dinosaurs did not all live at the same time. Different kinds of dinosaurs lived at different times.

DINO BITE:

When dinosaurs lived on Earth, all of the continents were pushed together in what is called Pangaea (say it like this: pan-JEE-uh).

Europe and Asia

North America

Africa

South America

India

Antarctica

Australia

Pangaea

There were no polar ice caps during the Age of Dinosaurs.

THE AGE OF DINOSAURS

Triassic Period (say it like this: tri-AS-sik)
About 230 million years ago, it was hot and dry. There were a lot of bugs, lizards, frogs, and dinosaurs!

Jurassic Period (say it like this: ju-RAS-sik)
Huge plant-eating dinosaurs roamed the Earth 210 million years ago. The oceans were full of fish and the **pterosaurs** (say it like this: TER-o-sores) ruled the skies. It was hot and dry, but it started to flood as the **continents** broke up.

**Cretaceous Period
(say it like this: kri-TAY-sheus)**
About 65 million years ago, it was a great time to be a dinosaur. There was a lot to eat. But there were a lot of **earthquakes** and **volcanoes**, too!

There were a lot of different kinds of dinosaurs.

 Some dinosaurs walked on two legs. Others walked on four legs. And some could do both.

Some dinosaurs were some dinosaurs that were very fast and some were slow.

 Some dinosaurs were covered with **armored** plates. Other dinosaurs had horns, crests, spikes, or frills.

Some had thick, bumpy skin. Others may have had feathers.

Dinosaurs could not fly and did not live in the water.

DINO BITE:

Some scientists think a big rock from space hit the Earth and caused a change in the climate. The dinosaurs could not live with this change.

Tyrannosaurus rex

(say it like this: tie-RAN-oh-SORE-us rex)

- T. rex could eat up to 500 pounds (230 kg) of meat and bones with one bite!

- A Tyrannosaurus rex's arms were very small, only 3 feet (1 m) long.

- The skin of a Tyrannosaurus rex was bumpy, like an alligator.

DINO FAST FACTS

Name means: tyrant lizard king

Lived: Late Cretaceous period

Size: 40 feet (12.2 m) long, more than 15 feet (4.6 m) tall

Food: meat; ate large dinosaurs

Fossils found: Western North America and Mongolia

Small T. rex tooth!

DINO BITE:
One T. rex fossil was found with teeth that were 13 inches (33 cm) long!

Stegosaurus

(say it like this: STEG-oh-SORE-us)

- Stegosaurus had 17 bony plates on its back and spikes on its tail.

- Scientists think Stegosaurus walked on all four legs.

- Stegosaurus was prey to large meat-eaters, like Allosaurus (say it like this: al-oh-SORE-us).

DINO FAST FACTS

Name means: roof lizard

Lived: Late Jurassic period

Size: more than 26 feet (8 m) long, 9 feet (2.75 m) tall at the hip

Food: plant-eater; ate ferns, moss, grass, and bushes

Fossils found: North America, India, Africa, and China

DINO BITE:

Stegosaurus' brain was the size of a walnut.

HELLO!

Baryonyx

(say it like this: BAR-ee-ON-iks)

- Baryonyx was smart compared to other dinosaurs.

- The front legs of Baryonyx were shorter than the back legs. It may have switched off walking on two to four legs.

- Baryonyx had powerful, crocodile-like jaws with 96 sharp teeth.

DINO FAST FACTS

Name means: heavy claw

Lived: Early Cretaceous period

Size: more than 32 feet (9.8 m) long, 8 feet (2.5 m) tall at the hip

Food: meat-eater; ate fish and young plant-eating dinosaurs

Fossils found: Europe

DINO BITE: Baryonyx is the only dinosaur known to have eaten fish.

The claws on its hands were 12 inches (30.5 cm) long!

Brachiosaurus

(say it like this: BRAK-e-oh-SORE-us)

- Brachiosaurus was one of the tallest and largest dinosaurs.

- Brachiosaurus probably traveled in herds, like horses or cows.

- Predators could get whipped by Brachiosaurus' long tail.

DINO FAST FACTS

Name means: arm lizard

Lived: Late Jurassic period

Size: more than 80 feet (24 m) long, 40 feet (12 m) tall at the head

Food: plant-eater; ate leaves and branches from trees

Fossils found: North America, Africa, and Europe

The nostrils on top of Brachiosaurus' head show it may have had a good sense of smell.

DINO BITE:

The front legs were longer than the back, but it walked on all four legs.

Coelophysis

(say it like this: SEE-low-FIE-sis)

- Coelophysis is one of the earliest-known dinosaurs.

- Coelophysis probably lived and hunted in packs, like wolves.

- It is thought that Coelophysis ran very fast on its two hind legs.

- Coelophysis had three clawed fingers on its hands.

DINO FAST FACTS

Name means: hollow form

Lived: Late Triassic period

Size: 9 feet (2.8 m) long, 3.5 feet (1 m) tall at the head

Food: meat-eater; ate small reptiles, and maybe other Coelophysis

Fossils found: North America

14

DINO BITE:

A Coelophysis skull went into space on Space Shuttle Endeavor.

15

Allosaurus

(say it like this: al-oh-SORE-us)

 Allosaurus had an S-shaped neck.

The claws on Allosaurus were 6 inches (15 cm) long.

 Scientists think Allosaurus may have hunted in groups.

Allosaurus walked on two legs.

DINO FAST FACTS

Name means: different lizard
Lived: Late Jurassic period
Size: about 40 feet (12 m) long, 10 feet (3 m) tall at the hip
Food: meat-eater; ate plant-eating dinosaurs
Fossils found: Western United States, Europe, Africa, and Australia

Allosaurus footprint

Ankylosaurus

(say it like this: ang-KIH-lo-SORE-us)

- Scientists believe that Ankylosaurus produced a lot of gas from eating tough plants.

- Ankylosaurus was built like a tank with bony plates, spikes on its body, horns on its head, and a club-like tail.

- Ankylosaurus had to defend itself against Tyrannosaurus rex and Deinonychus.

Name means: fused lizard
Lived: Late Cretaceous period
Size: more than 25 feet (7.6 m) long, 4 feet (1.2 m) tall at the hip
Food: plant-eater; ate low-lying plants
Fossils found: North America

DINO BITE:

Ankylosaurus walked on four short legs.

Velociraptor

(say it like this: vuh-LOSS-ih-RAP-tor)

Scientists think velociraptor may have been able to run up to 40 mph (64 Kph).

Some of velociraptor's 80 teeth were more than 1 inch (2.5 cm) long.

It is thought that velociraptor was one of the smarter dinosaurs.

DINO FAST FACTS

Name means: speedy thief
Lived: Late Cretaceous period
Size: more than 5 feet (1.5 m) long, 3 feet (1 m) tall at the hip
Food: meat-eater; ate plant-eating dinosaurs
Fossils found: Mongolia, Russia, and China

velociraptor had one deadly 3.5-inch (9-cm) long **retractable** claw on each foot.

Triceratops

(say it like this: try-SER-a-tops)

- This rhinoceros-like dinosaur walked on four legs.

- Triceratops' top horns were more than 3 feet (1 m) in length.

- When Triceratops was attacked, it might have charged like a modern-day rhinoceros.

DINO FAST FACTS

Name means: three-horned face

Lived: Late Cretaceous period

Size: about 30 feet (9 m) long, 7 feet (2 m) tall at the hips

Food: plant-eater; ate plants on or near the ground

Fossils found: Western North America

Deinonychus

(say it like this: die-NON-eye-cuss)

- Deinonychus ran fast on two legs.

- Each foot had 5-inch (13 cm) **Sickle-Shaped** claws.

- Deinonychus used its tail for balance and turning quickly.

- Deinonychus was one of the smartest dinosaurs.

DINO FAST FACTS

Name means: terrible claw

Lived: Cretaceous period

Size: about 10 feet (3 m) long, 5 feet (1.5 m) tall

Food: meat-eater; ate plant-eating dinosaurs

Fossils found: Western United States

HELLO!

24

Deinonychus may have hunted in groups, like modern-day wolves.

Gallimimus

(say it like this: gal-i-MY-muss)

- Gallimimus had hollow bones.
- The stiff tail helped Gallimimus turn fast.
- Gallimimus had comblike plates in its mouth for straining food from mud.
- Gallimimus was a birdlike dinosaur with a toothless beak.

DINO FAST FACTS

Name means: rooster mimic
Lived: Late Cretaceous period
Size: more than 13 feet (4 m) long, 6 feet (2 m) tall at the hip
Food: meat- and plant-eater; ate small lizards, insects, eggs, and some plants
Fossils found: Mongolia

Scientists think that Gallimimus could run up to 43 miles per hour (70 kph), like an ostrich.

Fossilized Skull Found!

On Monday, the fossilized skull of Gallimimus was found in Mongolia.

27

Anatotitan

(say it like this: a-NAT-o-TIE-tan)

- Anatotitan could walk on all fours but sometimes walked on two legs.

- They lived in herds, like cows today.

- Anatotitan was a duck-billed dinosaur.

- Anatotitan had cheek pouches and closely-packed teeth.

DINO FAST FACTS

Name means: giant duck

Lived: Late Cretaceous period

Size: about 33 feet (10 m) long, 8 feet (2.5 m) tall at the hip

Food: plant-eater; ate pine needles, twigs, seeds, and other plants

Fossils found: Northern United States

Sharks' teeth are replaced, too!

DINO BITE:

Anatotitan had a total of **720** teeth. If one broke, another replaced it.

29

Apatosaurus

(say it like this: a-PAT-oh-SORE-us)

- Apatosaurus walked on four legs but moved slowly.

- The eggs of Apatosaurus were huge at 12 inches (30 cm) wide.

- One toe on each foot had a thumb claw, which may have been used for protection.

DINO FAST FACTS
Name means: deceptive lizard
Lived: Late Jurassic period
Size: more than 70 feet (21 m) long, 10 feet (3 m) tall at the hips
Food: plant-eater; ate conifers, ferns, palmlike trees, and grasses
Fossils found: Western United States

Apatosaurus used to be called Brontosaurus.

Apatosaurus swallowed plants and leaves whole and may have swallowed **gastroliths** (say it like this: GAS-troh-liths) to help digest the plants.

31

Seismosaurus

- Like Apatosaurus and Brachiosaurus, Seismosaurus held its neck level to the ground.

- Scientists believe that Seismosaurus had a **lifespan** of 100 years.

- Seismosaurus moved very slowly on four legs.

DINO FAST FACTS

Name means: quake lizard

Lived: Late Jurassic period

Size: more than 130 feet (39 m) long, 18 feet (5.5 m) tall at the hip

Food: plant-eater; ate leaves, mosses, ferns, and grasses

Fossils found: Western United States

32

DINO BITE:

Seismosaurus is the longest dinosaur ever discovered.

The blue whale is bigger than any of the dinosaurs!

Troodon

(say it like this: TROH-oh-don)

- Scientists think Troodon may have eaten plants, as well as meat.

- Troodon had a large brain for its size. It may have been very smart.

- Troodon ran very fast on two legs.

DINO FAST FACTS

Name means: wounding tooth
Lived: Late Cretaceous period
Size: more than 6.5 feet (2 m) long, 12 inches (30 cm) tall at the hips
Food: meat-eater; ate just about anything
Fossils found: North America

DINO BITE:

The long, sharp teeth and claws helped Troodon capture prey.

Eoraptor

(say it like this: EE-oh-RAP-tor)

- Its two long back legs helped Eoraptor run fast.

- Eoraptor had a long head with a lot of small, sharp teeth.

- There were five fingers on each of Eoraptor's hands. Two of the fingers were very short.

DINO FAST FACTS

Name means: dawn thief
Lived: Late Triassic period
Size: about 3 feet (1 m) long, 5 feet (1.5 m) tall
Food: meat-eater; ate other dinosaurs and carrion
Fossils found: South America

36

Eoraptor is one of the earliest-known dinosaurs.

UPDATE

On the island of Madagascar, a newly discovered dinosaur is even older than Eoraptor at 230 million years old!

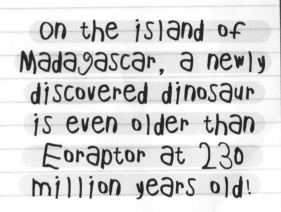

Maiasaura

(say it like this: my-ah-SORE-ah)

- Maiasaura was called a duck-billed dinosaur. Its flat skull looked like a duck's bill.

- Scientists think Maiasaura may have cared for its young.

- Newly hatched Maiasaura babies were about 12 inches (30 cm) long.

DINO FAST FACTS

Name means: good mother lizard
Lived: Late Cretaceous period
Size: about 30 feet (9 m) long, 6 feet (2 m) tall
Food: plant-eater; ate about 200 pounds (90.7 kg) of leaves, berries, and seeds each day
Fossils found: Northwestern North America

Maiasaura fossils were found in groups of about 10,000, which suggests they traveled in herds and may have **migrated**.

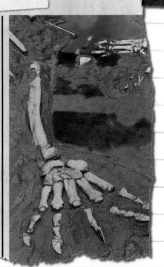

A Maiasaura nest was a hole scooped out of the ground.

Giganotosaurus

(say it like this: jig-a-NOT-oh-SORE-us)

- The longest meat-eating dinosaur yet discovered is the Giganotosaurus.

- Giganotosaurus was probably bigger than Tyrannosaurus rex.

- The Giganotosaurus had knife-like teeth that sliced.

DINO FAST FACTS

Name means: giant southern reptile
Lived: Mid-Cretaceous period
Size: more than 44 feet (13.5 m) long, 13 feet (3.9 m) tall at the hips
Food: meat-eater; ate large, plant-eating dinosaurs
Fossils found: South America

DINO BITE:

Scientists think Giganotosaurus' brain was banana-shaped.

41

Microraptor

(say it like this: MY-cro-RAP-tor)

- Microraptor fossils have been found with impressions of feathers and four wings.

- The four wings, one on each of Microraptor's forelegs and hind legs, helped it glide, but it didn't fly.

- Some scientists think Microraptor may have lived in trees.

DINO FAST FACTS

Name means: small thief

Lived: Early Cretaceous period

Size: about 2 feet (61 cm) long, 5 feet (1.5 m) tall

Food: meat-eater; probably ate small lizards and insects

Fossils found: China

42

DINO BITE:

Microraptor is one of the smallest-known dinosaurs.

Microraptor was discovered in 2003.

Tawa hallae

(say it like this: ta-WAH hall-A)

- One specimen is a nearly complete skeleton of a young Tawa hallae.

- Its body was about the size of a dog, but with a much longer tail.

- Tawa hallae's brain and neck were surrounded by airsacs, like modern-day birds.

HELLO!

DINO FAST FACTS

Name means: named after the **Hopi** word for the Pueblo sun god and Ruth Hall

Lived: Late Triassic period

Size: about 6.5 to 13 feet (2 to 4 m) long; 3 to 5 feet (1 to 1.5 m) tall at the hips

Food: most likely a meat-eater

Fossils found: New Mexico, USA

44

Tawa hallae fossils were found in 2009.

45

Draw your own Dinosaur

Glossary

Armored: covered with hard, protective plates

Carrion: the meat of a dead animal

Continents: the large areas of land on Earth

Cretaceous period: a length of time 145-65 million years ago, it was the last time dinosaurs lived on Earth

Dinosaur: "terrible lizard," these were reptiles that lived on land for 165 million years

Earthquake: shaking at the surface of the Earth caused by underground movement

Extinct: when an entire species of animal or plant no longer lives on Earth

Fossil: the remains or evidence of any creature that once lived on Earth

Gastroliths: literally means "stomach stones," these were stones that some plant-eating dinosaurs swallowed to help them digest their food